The Language of the
Dakota or Sioux Indians

By Frederic Louis Otto Rœhrig

From the Report of the Smithsonian Institution for 1871

Adansonia
Press

Logo art adapted from work by Bernard Gagnon

ISBN-13: 978-0-359-74703-0

First published in 1872

Contents

The Language of the Dakota or Sioux Indians

In the year 1866 the writer of this article spent the interval from the 4th of July to the 26th of November in constant intercourse with the Dakota or Sioux Indians, near Fort Wadsworth, Northern Dakota Territory.

Previously to his going to that out-of-the-way region he had happened to make himself in some measure acquainted with the languages of several of the Indian tribes, particularly with the Chippewa tongue; and he then at once directed his attention to the language of those Indians in whose immediate neighborhood he was going to reside for a while, namely, the *Sioux Nation*, or *Dakotas.*

It would take a whole volume to record his varied experience with those interesting tribes and the result of his ethnological and linguistic researches during the time he lived among them. On this occasion, however, he will content himself with presenting to the reader only a very few faint and cursory glimpses of merely such matters as may arise in his recollection, and as pertain to the language of these people. It is hoped that his elucidation of desultory topics of this nature will not prove altogether uninteresting to the ethnologist or philological inquirer.

Whenever any new truth is presented for our comprehension, or any new subject for our study and investigation, almost invariably the first thing for the human mind to do, and that, too, from an inherent craving for logical classification, is to inquire as to what other known truth the less known can possibly be linked; to what chain or series of analogous phenomena it necessarily belongs; in what accredited system it has to take its place; with what whole or totality it is connected as a part; and we seem never to be fairly at ease before we have arrived at the point of grouping or classifying the matter in some way or other. This applies also and particularly to *languages.* As soon as a new language begins to attract our attention, we feel at once an eager desire to classify it, so much so that we often cannot patiently wait even during the time necessary to collect the indispensable material from which alone we could possibly draw any legitimate conclusions in this respect. We at once ask what other tongue such language is like; with what other it maybe compared; where among the languages of the world it has to take its place, &c., and hence the often over-hasty classifications based upon mere casual and apparent resemblances. It is first of all necessary, in such cases, to be able fairly to survey a language in all its relations; in its manifold diversities, its dialects, and, if possible, also in its various and successive phases of development, in its primary forms or its original condition.

So far as we know, the Dakota language, with several cognate tongues, constitutes a separate class or family among American Indian languages, of which we may speak on some other occasion. But the question at present is, whence does the Dakota, with its related American tongues, come? From what trunk or parent stock is it derived? Ethnologists are wont to point us to Asia as the most probable source of the prehistorical immigration from the Old World to this continent. Hence, they say, many if not all of our Indians must have come from Eastern or Middle Asia, and in considering their respective tongues, one must still find somewhere in that region some cognate, though perhaps very remotely related set of languages, however much the affinity existing between the Indian tongues and these may have gradually become obscured, and in how many instances soever, through a succession of ages, the old family features may have been impaired. But they further allow, of course, that these changes may have taken place to such an extent that this affinity cannot be easily recognized, and may be much, even altogether, obliterated.

When we consider the languages of the great Asiatic continent, of its upper and eastern portions more particularly, with a view of discovering any remaining trace, however faint, of analogy with or similarity to the *Dakota* tongue, what do we find? Very little; and the only group of Asiatic languages in which we could *possibly* fancy we perceived any kind of dim and vague resemblance, an occasional analogy or other perhaps *merely casual* coincidence with the Sioux or Dakota tongue, would probably be the so-called "Ural-Altaic" family. This group embraces a very wide range, and is found scattered in manifold ramifications through parts of Eastern, Northern, and Middle Asia, extending in some of its more remote branches even to the heart of Europe, where the Hungarian and the numerous tongues of the far-spread Finnish tribes offer still the same characteristics, and an unmistakable impress of the old Ural-Altaic relationship.

In the following pages we shall present some isolated glimpses of such resemblances, analogies, &c., with the Sioux language as strike us, though we need not repeat that no conclusions whatever can be drawn from them regarding any affinity, ever so remote, between the Ural-Altaic languages and the Dakota tongue. This much, however, may perhaps be admitted from what we have to say, that at least an *Asiatic origin* of the Sioux or Dakota Nation and their language may not be altogether an impossibility.

In the first place, we find that as in those Ural-Altaic languages, so in a like manner in the Sioux or Dakota tongue, there exists that remarkable syntactical structure of sentences which we might call a constant *inversion* of the mode and order in which *we* are accustomed to think. Thus, more or less, the people who speak those languages would *begin* sentences or periods where we *end* ours, so that our thoughts would really appear in their mind as *inverted.*

Those Asiatic languages have, moreover, no *preposi*-tions, but only *post*positions. So likewise has the Dakota tongue.

The *polysynthetic* arrangement which prevails throughout the majority of the American Indian languages is less prominent, and decidedly less intricate in the Dakota tongue than in those of the other tribes of this continent. But it may be safely asserted that the above-mentioned languages of Asia also contain at least a similar polysynthetic *tendency,* though merely in an incipient state, a *rudimental* or partially developed form. Thus, for instance, all the various modifications which the fundamental meaning of a verb has to undergo, such as passive condition, causation, reflexive action, mutuality, and the like, are embodied in the verb itself by means of interposition, or a sort of intercalation of certain characteristic syllables between the root and the grammatical endings of such verb, whereby a long-continued and united series, or catenation, is often obtained, forming apparently one huge word. However, to elucidate this any further here would evidently lead us too far away from our present subject and purpose. We only add that postpositions, pronouns, as well as the interrogative particle, &c., are also commonly blended into one with the nouns, by being inserted one after the other, where several such expressions occur, in the manner alluded to, the whole being closed by the grammatical terminations, so as often to form words of considerable length. [1] May we not feel authorized to infer from this some sort of approach, in however feeble a degree, of those Asiatic languages - through this principle of catenation - to the general polysynthetic system of the American tongues?

We now proceed to a singular phenomenon, which we should like to describe technically as a sort of *"reduplicatio intensitiva."* It exists in the Mongolian and Turco-Tartar branches of the Ural-Altaic group, and some vestiges of it we found, to our great surprise, also in the language of our Sioux Indians.

This reduplication is in the above-mentioned Asiatic languages applied particularly to adjectives denoting *color* and *external qualities,* and it is just the same in the Dakota language. It consists in prefixing to any given word its first syllable in the shape of a reduplication, this syllable thus occurring twice — often adding to it (as the case may be) a *"p,"* &c.

The object — at least in the Asiatic languages alluded to — is to express thereby, in many cases, a higher degree or increase of the quality. An example or two will make it clear. Thus we have, for instance, in Mongolian, *khara,* which means *black,* and KHAp-khara with the meaning of *very black, entirely Mack; tsagan, white,* TSAp-*tsagan, entirely white,* &c., and in the Turkish and the so-called Tartar (Tatar) dialects of Asiatic Russia, *kara, black,* and KAP-*kara, very black; sary, yellow,* and SAP-*sary, entirely yellow,* &c.

Now, in Dakota, we find *sapa. black,* and with the reduplication, Sap-*sapa.* The reduplication here is, indeed, a reduplication of the syllable *sa,* and not of *sap,* the word being *sa*-pa, and not *sap*-a. The *"p"* in SAP-*sapa* is inserted after the reduplication of the first syllable, just as we have seen in the above *kara* and KAP-*kara,* &c.

In the Ural-Altaic languages "*m*" also is sometimes inserted after the first syllable; for instance, in the Turkish *beyaz, white,* and BEM-*beyaz, very white,* &c. If we find, however, similar instances in the Dakota language, such as *cepa,* [2] which means *fleshy,* (one of the *external* qualities to which this rule applies,) and ćEm-ćepa, &c., we must consider that the letter "*m*" is in such cases merely a contraction, and replaces, moreover, another labial letter ("*p*") followed by a vowel, particularly "*a.*" Thus, for instance, ćo*m* is a contraction for ćo*pa*, ga*m* for ga*pa*, ha*m* for ha*pa*, ske*m* for ske*pa*, o*m* for o*pa*, to*m* for to*pa*, &c. So is će*m*, in our example, only an abridged form of će*pa*; hence "*m*" stands here for "*p*" or "*pa,*" and belongs essentially to *the word itself,* while in those Asiatic languages the "*m*" is *added* to the reduplication of the first syllable, like the "*p*" in KAP-*kara,* &c. We have, therefore, to be very careful in our conclusions.

The simple doubling of the first syllable is also of frequent occurrence in Dakota; for instance, *gi, brown,* and *gigi,* (same meaning;) *sni, cold,* and *snisni; ko, quick,* and *koko,* &c.

There are also some very interesting examples to be found in the Dakota language, which strikingly remind us of a remarkable peculiarity frequently met with in the Asiatic languages above adverted to. It consists in the *antagonism* in *form,* as well as in *meaning,* of certain words, according to the nature of their *vowels;* so that when such words contain what we may call the strong, full, or hard vowels, viz: *a, o, u,* (in the continental pronunciation,) they generally denote *strength,* the *male* sex, *affirmation, distance,* &c., while the same words with the weak or soft vowels *c, i,* — the consonantal *skeleton, frame,* or *groundwork of the word remaining the same,* — express *weakness,* the *female* sex, *negation, proximity,* and a whole series of corresponding ideas.

A few examples will demonstrate this. Thus, for instance, the idea of "*father*" is expressed in Mantchoo (one of the Ural-Altaic languages) by *ama,* while "*mother*" is *eme.* [3] This gives, no doubt, but a very incomplete idea of that peculiarity, but it will, perhaps, be sufficient to explain in a measure what we found analogous in the Dakota language. Instances of the kind are certainly of rare occurrence in the latter, and we will content ourselves with giving here only a very few examples, in which the above difference of signification is seen to exist, though the significance of the respective vowels seems to be just the reverse; which would in no wise invalidate the truth of the preceding statement, since the same inconsistent alteration or anomaly frequently takes place also in the family of Ural-Altaic languages. (For further developments, see the Notes at the end of this article.)

Thus we find in the Dakota or Sioux *language,* hEpan, (second *son* of a family,) and hApan, (second *daughter* of a family;) ćIn, elder *brother,* ćUŋ, *elder sister;* [4] ćIŋksi, *son,* ćUŋksi, *daughter,* &c. Also the demonstrative kOn, *that,* and kIn, *this, the,* (the definite articles,) seem to come, in some respects, under this head.

To investigate the grammatical structure of languages from a comparative point of view is, however, but one part of the work of the philologist; the other equally essential part consists in the study of the words themselves, the very material of which languages are made. We do not, as yet, intend to touch on the question of Dakota words and their possible affinities, but reserve all that pertains to comparative etymology for some other time. The identity of words in different languages, or simply their affinity, may be either immediately recognized, or rendered evident by a regular process of philological reasoning, especially when such words appear, as it were, disguised, in consequence of certain alterations due to time and to various vicissitudes, whereby either the original vowels, or the consonants, or both, have become changed. Then, also, it frequently happens that one and the same word, when compared in cognate languages, may appear as different parts of speech, so that in one of them it may exist as a noun, and in another only as a verb, &c. Moreover, the same word may have become gradually modified in its original meaning, so that it denotes, for instance, in one of the cognate languages, the *genus,* and in another, merely the *species* of the same thing or idea. Or it may also happen that when several synonymous expressions originally existed in what we may call a *mother* language, they have become so scattered in their descent that only one of these words is found in a certain *one* of the derived languages; while others again belong to *other* cognate tongues, or even their dialects, exclusively.

The foregoing is sufficient to account for the frequent failures in establishing the relationship of certain languages in regard to the affinity of all their *words.*

On this occasion it will be enough to mention, in passing, as it were, one or two of the most frequently used words, such as the names of *father, mother,* &c.

In regard to these most familiar expressions, we again find a surprising coincidence between the tongues of Upper Asia (or more extensively viewed, the Ural-Altaic or Tartar-Finnish stock of languages) and the Dakota.

Father is in Dakota *ate*; in Tuixo-Tartar, *ata*; Mongolian and its branches, etsä, *etsige*; in the Finnish languages we meet with the forms *attje, atä,* &c.; they all having *at* (= *et*) as their radical syllable. Now, as to *mother,* it is in the Dakota language *ina;* and in the Asiatic tongues just mentioned it is *ana, aniya, ine, eniye,* &c.

Again, we find in the Dakota or Sioux language *tanin,* which means *to appear,* to be *risible, manifest, distinct, clear.* Now, we have also in all the Tartar dialects *tan, tang,* which means, 1st, *light;* hence, *dawn* of the morning; 2d, *understanding.* From it is derived *tani,* which is the stem or radical part of verbs meaning to *render manifest, to make known, to know;* it also appears in the old Tartar verb-stems *tang-(la),* meaning *to understand,* and in its mutilated modern (and western) form, *ang(la),* without the initial "*t,*" which has the same signification. We may mention still *mama,* which in Dakota denotes the *female breast.* We might compare it with the Tartar *meme,* which has the same meaning, if we had not also in almost all Eu-

13

ropean languages the word *mamma,* (= *mama,*) with the very same fundamental signification, the children of very many different nations calling their mothers, instinctively, as it were, by that name, (*mamma* = *mama,* &c.) [5]

We may also assert that even in the *formation* of words we find now and then some slight analogy between certain characteristic endings in the languages of Upper Asia and the Dakota tongue. Thus, for instance, the termination for the "*nomen agens,*" which in the Dakota language is *sa,* is in Tartar *tsi, si,* and *dchi;* Mongolian *tchi,* &c. We also find in Dakota the postposition *ta,* (a constituent part of ekta, *in, at,*) which is a locative particle, and corresponds in form to the postpositions *ta* and *da,* and their several varieties and modifications, in the greater part of the Ural-Altaic family of languages. The same remark applies in a measure to the Dakota postposition *e,* which means *to, toward,* &c. [6]

In pointing out these various resemblances of the Sioux language to Asiatic tongues we in no wise mean to say that we are inclined to believe in any affinity or remote relationship among them. At this early stage of our researches it would be wholly preposterous to make any assertions as to the question of affinity, &c. All that we intended to do was simply to bring forward a few facts from which, if they should be *further corroborated* by a more frequent recurrence of the phenomena here touched upon, the reader might *perhaps* draw his own conclusions, at least so far as a *very remote* Asiatic *origin* of the Dakota language is concerned. Further investigations in the same direction might possibly lead to more satisfactory results.

After having hitherto considered the Dakota or Sioux language somewhat in connection with other tongues, we shall now say a word more about that language viewed *independently,* in its own natural growth and development.

Vowel changes, although far less important in themselves than consonantal permutations, occur very abundantly in the Dakota language. Changes of that kind bear to each other nearly the same relation that the English "*and*" bears to the German "*und,*" &c., only that those forms exist, and are contemporaneously used, in one and the same language. Thus, for instance, the Dakota Indians call the Iowa tribe "*ayúhba,*" as well as "*iyúhba,*" (the sleepers); the verb *"to mind"* is in Dakota "*awaćin*" as well as "*ewaćin;*" "*yukanpi,*" aswell as "*yakonpi,*"is used to express *are,* (of the verb *"to be"*) We have also double forms of words, differing only in the vowel they contain, such as kpa, kpe, (*lasting, durable,* &c.;) kta, kte, (*to kill;*) spa, spe, &c.

Sometimes, however, the difference of a vowel occasions also some slight modification in the meaning; for instance, *o*nataka and *i*nataka, both implying the same idea, only the former being the verb, the latter the noun; wowinihan, *awe;* wawipihan, *awful;* ośkopa, *areh;* and aśkopa, *arched,* &c.

In the Dakota language, we must add, it is of the highest importance that the philologist should, when comparing words with different vowels, be exceedingly careful not to see in them always merely double forms of one and the same expression. For, in this language it often happens that syllables which differ only in their vowels are nevertheless sometimes of an essentially different origin, and may denote ideas wholly heterogeneous, and thus enter as parts into compounds in all else similar to each other. Thus, for instance, wada s'a means a beggar; woda s'a means the same. Nevertheless, they are different compounds, the former meaning simply *one who asks for something, who begs,* while the first syllable of the latter, namely, *wo,* is an entirely different word from *wa,* and means *food;* so that woda s'a alludes to *begging food, begging for something to eat.* Equal caution is necessary when comparing words like the following, which in their constituent parts are by no means identical, viz: yawaśte and yuwaśte, both meaning *to bless.* They have both the word *waśte, good,* in common; but ya-waśte means literally *to call good,* and yu-waśte *to make good.* The same is the case with yatanin and yutanin, which means *to disclose;* yaonihan aud yuonihan, *to glorify;* yahepa and yuhepa; *to imbibe,* and a great many others.

We close these remarks with a few words on the harmonious character of this language. Vowels undergo changes not only for the purpose of expressing various modifications of the original meaning, but also for mere euphonic reasons. There is, in fact, a greater tendency in the Dakota language to bring about a constantly harmonious, smooth, graceful, and easy flow of speech than in almost any other of the known Indian tongue. Thus, we frequently find the vowel *a*, for the sake of euphony, changed to *e*; and for the same reason, any possible hiatus carefully avoided by elisions, while semi-vowels are frequently inserted where two vowels would otherwise come into immediate contact with each other and impair the harmoniousness of the sound. Contractions are also used for the same purpose, and the accent or stress of voice moves, according to certain laws, from one syllable to the other in the inflectional changes which a word undergoes, whereby the language becomes often very pleasing and majestic. Indeed, if a comparison were allowed of the widely-different but far more flexible and varied Chippewa, and our more slowly-moving, grave, and manly Dakota language, we would venture to compare, as far as euphony and sonorousness are concerned, the former with the Greek and the latter with the Latin language. In regard to the accent, we may also mention that in some instances difference of accentuation in a word is, in Dakota, resorted to as a means of distinguishing homophonous expressions with different meanings, such as, for instance, would be in 'English *presént* and to *presént* or in German "gébet," (give ye,) and " gebét," (prayer;) or in Greek ϑεότοχος and ϑεοτόχος, &c. Thus, in Dakota, *húta* means the *root of a tree or plant,* while *hutá* denotes the *shore of a river or lake,* also the *edge of a prairie or wood.* Consonants also often undergo changes merely for the sake of *euphony;* thus, gutturals become palatals, and the change of *k* to *ć* (tch) is of frequent occurrence, though in all such cases care is taken not to obscure thereby the indication of any etymological changes which words may have undergone, either by combination or inflection.

We often find double forms of a word simultaneously existing, one of them, however, being the older, the more complete; the other, the more recent but already decaying and impaired form, which finally will supersede the former, and remain alone in use. Thus, to give a simple instance, chosen from a great number of similar examples, frequently very complex, intricate, and obscure, *wipi,* in Dakota, means *full;* but in the coexisting form, *ipi, full,* the "*w*" has already begun to disappear, although both forms, *wipi* and *ipi,* are used, and will be until the former (*w*ipi) becomes by degrees obsolete. [7] Other instances are, w*oniya* and *oniya,* (*breath;*) w*ipata* and *ipata,* (*ornament;*) w*ihdi* and *ihdi,* (*grease, ointment;*) *woźuha* and *oźuha,* (*a bag,*) &c. We mast, however, be very careful not to mistake the significance of "*w*" in such forms where, in one, its presence constitutes simply an addition to the word, a sort of formative prefix, and, in the other, its absence is in nowise an elision, for it is frequently found used as an element in the formation of certain derivatives or compounds. Thus, for instance, the prefix "*wa*" before a word commencing with a vowel becomes reduced to a simple "*w*" in consequence of the elision of "*a,*" for euphonic reasons. It may also happen that the "*w*" serves to distinguish certain modifications in the meaning of a word, so that the two forms, though closely related, can no longer be considered as altogether identical. Instances of this kind are, w*opeton* and op*eton,* two verbs which are, indeed, often confounded with each other, and used indiscriminately to express *trading;* while, however, strictly speaking, *opeton* means *to purchase, to buy, to hire,* and w*opeton, to buy,* but also *to buy and sell, to trade. Wowa, to paint, to write,* forms, by the addition of "*pi,*" the usual ending of verbal nouns, the word *wowapi,* which means a *writing,* a *book;* while *owapi* means more particularly a *picture,* something that is *painted* or *lettered,* though these differences do not always seem to be kept distinct, *wowapi* being, in the Dakota dialects, used also for *painting, picture,* for a *letter,* a *sheet of paper,* &c. The letter "*h,*" at the beginning of words, frequently disappears likewise; thus we have the doable forms H*i* and *i,* (*to come;*) Hećoŋ and ećoŋ, (to do;) Hnaśka and *naśka,* (*a frog;*) Hećen and e*ćen,* (*such as,*) &c. We also find, in some instances, that consonants are dropped at the end of words, as in the double forms *hektaM* and *hekta,* (*back,*) &c.; "*k*" also disappears not unfrequently, which accounts for the double forms K*u* and *u,* (to come,) &c. *K* may disappear also in the middle of words; thus we have *kaKi* and *kai,* (*to carry,*) &c. It sometimes happens that when "*k,*" in the middle of a word, is followed by "*i,*" this syllable "*ki*" is dropped; hence, we have double forms, such as iKIuŋ and iuŋ (*to anoint;*) iiKIyuwi and iiyuwi, (*to bridle,*) &c. But the greatest care is necessary not to confound this "*ki*" with the grammatical syllable "*ki,*" which is inserted in verbs to impart to them a more definite meaning, and is particularly incorporated in verbs indicating a special relation *to* or *for* whom anything is done; as, for instance, *oyaka*, (to tell;) *oKIyaka*, (to tell to one, to somebody;) thus, *omaKIyaka*, (tell me,) &c.

We have in the Dakota language also a very interesting system of *consonantal* permutations. Thus, among the *liquids*, a frequent (and often almost optional) interchange of *l* and *n*; for instance, *boy* is in the Dakota *hokśiLa* and *hokśiNa*, (*l* and *n*;) or, if we wish to compare the dialects of that language with one another, we have in Yanktonais *LiLa* for *"very;"* in the Titoŋ dialect the same; in Sissitoŋ *NiNa*, (*l* and *n* again interchanged.) Also the liquids n and m are interchangeable, often ad libitum, even within the limits of one and the same Dakota dialect; thus, for instance, the English preposition *"on," "upon,"* is in Dakota "aka*n*" as well as "aka*m*," &c.

We have in the Dakota language also a frequent interchange of *k* and *t*, [8] as, for instance, *iKpi* and *iTpi*, both forms being used to denote *belly, abdomen.* Thus, *ćeKpa*, which means *navel, twin,* may assume a double form in the compounds *hokśićeKpa* and *hokśićeTpa*, where *k* and *t* interchange with each other without affecting the signification of the word in any way whatever. Other examples are *oKpaza* and *oTpaza*, meaning *darkness, night; wiyaKpaKpa* and *wiyaTpaTpa*, signifying *to glisten, to glitter*, &c. This change takes place especially where the *k* or *t* is immediately followed by *p*. The permutation above adverted to, between *k* and *ć*, (*tch,*) is also of frequent occurrence. It not only takes place in consequence of certain euphonic laws, but it would seem to be also optional, as we find

20

double forms of one and the same word, the one with k, the other with ć; as, for instance, *iKute* and *ićute*, meaning *ammunition,* &c. *K* interchanges also with *y*, as, for instance, in the double forms *Kamna* and *Yamna*, meaning *to acquire,* &c. Then, again, *y* interchanges with ć; thus *hokśiYopa* and *hokśićopa,* [9] meaning *child. K* interchanges, moreover, with *p*; for instance, *Kasto* and *Pasto,* (*brush,*) &c. *K* interchanges also with *b*, as *Katoŋta* and *Batoŋta,* (*notch,*) &c. Then, we furthermore observe that labials interchange with each other; for instance, *b* with *p*, as *Bago* and *Pago*, two forms of one and the same verb, meaning *to carve.* Also, the labials *p* and *m* are seen to interchange with each other; thus, *naPkawiŋ* and *naMkawiŋ*, (*to beckon with the hand.*) &c. There are also instances of a permutation between *p* and *t,* such *petusPe* and *petusTe,* (*a fire-brand,*) &c. Also *t* and *ś* sometimes interchange with one another, as in *kTaŋ* and *kśan*, which mean *curved,* whence the compounds *yukTaŋ* and *yukśaŋ,* meaning literally *to make curved* or *to bend,* &c. It now and then happens that such consonantal interchanges take place, and are, moreover, accidentally *complicated* by a *transposition* of the consonants in question; for instance, *opTaye* and *ośPaye,* &c. It is important to take all these various changes into careful consideration when we wish to identify words in their different appearances, their innumerable protean transformations, and often surprising modes of disguise, and to trace their origin, derivation, and various affinities.

In regard to the derivation and composition of words, the Dakota or Sioux language is particularly clear and transparent. Derivations can be traced with great facility, and in the matter of the formation of compound words, this language is remarkably apt and flexible. We will take this opportunity to present but a few instances of Dakota etymologies, which will, however, be sufficient to enable the reader to form some idea of this particular subject. *Ti* means *to dwell, to live in,* and as a noun the same word means a *dwelling-place, a house.* With the addition of the substantive ending *pi,* (*tipi,*) it means a *tent,* such as the Sionx Indians inhabit; while when combined with the verb *opa,* which signifies *to go in, to enter, to go to,* it forms *tiyopa,* (for *tiopa,*) which is a substantive and designates *a door, a gate, an entrance. Da* is a verb which means to *form an opinion, to think;* its longer form is *daka,* with the same meaning. This word added to the adjective *waśte, good,* forms the compounds *waśteda* and *waśte-daka,* which mean *to deem good, to think well of;* hence, *to love.* On the contrary, when combined with *siće, bad,* it forms the compounds *sićeda* and *sićedaka,* which mean *to consider bad,* and, by a natural transition, *to hate.*

The word *hokśi* gives rise to a number of derivatives, of which we will here mention but a few. The word itself does not appear to be used independently; but we may, perhaps, infer its fundamental meaning, when we consider a compound expression like *hokśi-ćekpa,* which not only means *twins,* but, in its probably more original signification, applies to a flower, and denotes a *blue wild flower* which appears *first* in the *spring,* the *earliest spring-flower,* thus alluding to the first beginning of floral vegetation. In a similar acceptation, it seems to enter as the principal constituent part into all words expressive of the idea of *infancy* and *childhood,* as *hokśiyopa,* a child = *hokśiopa,* the verb *opa,* most probably, with its meaning of *following, going along with; hokśidaŋ,* a *boy, daŋ* being a very common diminutive termination, alluding here, it seems, simply to the youth and small stature of a male during childhood, &c.; *hokśiwiŋ* and *hokśiwiŋna,* a *virgin.* In the latter expression we distinguish in the ending the word *wiŋ,* that by itself means *female, woman,* and *wiŋna,* which is its diminutive, and stands to it somewhat in the same relation as the German *fraülein, a young unmarried woman,* to *frau, a woman.*

The word *gu* means to *burn; guya* is a causative form of *gu,* and means *to cause to burn, to make burn.* This word appears also, and, it seems, in a more definite sense, under the form *agu,* (with prefixed *a,*) to *burn,* and *aguya, to cause to burn.* With the usual substantive-ending of verbal nouns, viz: *pi, aguyapi,* means *bread,* as it were, something *burned* or *baked.* With a similar import the radical letters *br* in our English word *bread,* German *brod,* seem to refer to the same idea, as they appear also in BRennen, BRand, BRühen, BRauen, BRüten, BRüten, BRunst, &c., in all of which expressions the idea of heat, if not of fire, is evidently implied. [10]

Interrogatives, which also in this language coincide in their form with relative and indefinite pronouns, present here the peculiarity of commencing, in the greatest number of instances, with *t* or *d*, while the *demonstratives* begin with *k*. For example: T*uwe, who;* T*aku, what;* T*ohan, when;* T*ohaŋ, where;* T*ona, how many,* &c. And of the demonstratives we may mention K*a, that;* K*aki, there;* K*ana, these.* Sometimes we find also the *guttural* softened down to a simple *h*; as, for instance, H*ena,* the equivalent of K*ana, these;* H*ehaŋ,* which means *there,* and answers to the above-mentioned tohaŋ, *where;* and H*ehan,* which means *then,* and responds to *tohan, when.* We may observe here, by the way, that in most of the other languages which come under our ordinary observation precisely the contrary takes place, viz: *guttural* letters (which are also sometimes found replaced by their equivalent *labials*) serving to express the *interrogative;* while *t, d, th,* commonly occur in the demonstratives. Thus, we have in Latin *t*alis, *t*antus, *t*ot, *t*am, *t*um, *t*unc, &c.; in Greek, τό, τόσος, τότε &c.; in English, *t*his, *t*hat, *t*hus, *t*here, *t*hen, &c.; and with the gutturals, in Latin, *q*uis, *q*uid, *q*ualis, *q*uantus, *q*uot, *q*uam, *q*uum, &c.; in Greek dial., κῶς = πῶς; κότε = πότε; κότερος = πότερος &c. [11] The same phenomenon is remarked also, in a measure, in a great many other languages widely different from those last mentioned. We may state here, as a curious fact, that the *Dakota* mode of expressing the more essential part in *interrogatives* by *t* or *d,* and what corresponds thereto in *demonstratives* by *k,* obtains also in the language of Japan, where it constitutes indeed an eminently striking feature. It is true, *k* and *t* are interchangeable, and, in many instances, convertible elements in languages generally, but their functions are kept distinct and apart in the particular matter under consideration.

We pass on to the *Dakota* word *akan,* which means *above.* It is the same as *aka*M, and if not identical with, is at least related to *akaŋ*; just as we see, for instance, the double forms *kaha*N and *kahaŋ,* which mean *then, there, so far,* and one of which has *n* where the other has *ŋ*; that is, *n*, with only a *nasal pronunciation.* Now, the *akaŋ,* as an adjective, means also *old,* implying, no doubt, the idea of *above,* of *superior to,* (in *stature* or in *years,*) just as the Latin *alt*us reappears in the German *alt,* English *eld; old.* This *akaŋ,* or, *per aphoeresin,* simply *kaŋ,* appears also in the form of *wakaŋka,* [12] an *old* woman. *Akaŋ* reappears also under the forms (w)*akan* and *waŋkan,* meaning likewise *above, up, high, superior,* and being undoubtedly closely connected with the form (w)*akaŋ,* since *n* and *ŋ* are interchangeable terms, (as shown in the above *kaha*N and *kahaŋ*); and since certain derivates, moreover, are seen to confirm their intimate relationship, such as *wakaŋićidapi, pride, haughtiness,* where *wakaŋ* evidently refers to real or fancied superiority, similarly to the Latin *super*bus, the French *alt*ier, &c. Perhaps *wakapa* also comes under this head, its meaning being *to excel,* to *sur*pass, to be *superior* to, or to be *above; wakapa* standing, according to all appearance, for *wakaŋkapa,* the latter part of which would be the verb k*apa, to pass by, to go beyond.* Thus the primary and fundamental meaning of wakaŋ (=*akaŋ, akam, akan*) would be *what is superior* or *above, a superior* something or being; hence it means *a spirit, a ghost,* and, as an adjective, *spiritual, supernatural, divine.* It gives rise to the following expressions: *mini-wakaŋ,* which signifies *alcohol, brandy;* as it were, *spirit-water,* or *spirituous liquor;* [13] *wakaŋ tanka,* the *Great Spirit,* meaning God; *wakaŋ sića, evil spirit,* meaning *demon, devil; wowapi wakaŋ,* literally *spirit book,* or *spiritual, divine book,* the Dakota name for the Bible; *tipi-wakaŋ,* which means a *chapel* or *church,* literally *spirit house, sacred house; wićaste-wakaŋ* a *clergyman, priest,* literally a *spiritual man;* &c. Thus, also, the lightning is called *wakaŋhdi,* from *wakaŋ* (spirit) and *hdi,* (to come,) meaning, as it were, the coming down or arrival of a *spirit.* Also, the famous dance of the Sioux Indians, which is described as the Medicine-dance, viz: *wakaŋ waćipi,* simply means *spirit-dance* or *sacred dance,* and, as Rev. S. R. Riggs expressly informs us in his Dictionary, is thus called especially from the fact that the high priests of the ceremonies spend the night previous in singular magic practices, and are *holding communion with the spirit world.* Then, again, we have the word *wakaŋ* in compound verbs, such as *wakaŋ kago,* which means literally *to make wakaŋ,* as it were, *to attend the acts of worship or divine service;* and *wakaŋećong* means to perform *supernatural acts,* to do *tricks of jugglery,* of *magic.* A great error has been committed by travelers generally, who, resorting, perhaps for information, to the stolid half-breed Sioux Indians, who are often still more ignorant, if possible, of English than the travelers are of the Dakota tongue, have identified the idea expressed by the word *wakaŋ* and everything therewith connected with that of *the healing art,* or *medicine.* To be sure, *healing a disease,* restoring a sufferer from sickness to health, is in the opinion of the wild Indian always and pre-eminently a supernatural, wonderful act, in which beings of a higher order directly participate, and which is generally brought about by means of magical performances, conjuring, necromancy, and sorcery, rather than by the administration of remedies or other medical appliances. There is no such thing as a "*medicine man*" among these Indians, and they have not even a word for it; for *wićaśte-wakaŋ,* which has been erroneously taken for such, simply means a *supernatural man,* a *spirit man,* a *magician,* and the like, and has come subsequently to be applied to the *priest, clergyman,* or *missionary.* An Indian doctor is called *wapiye* among the Dakotas, which simply means a conjurer, and is derived from the verb *wapiya, to conjure the sick,* which in its turn comes from *pikiya, to conjure.* A physician, or one who cures diseases by means of *medicine,* is always called *peźihuta-wićaśte,* from *peźi,* which means *grass,* also *dry grass, herb,* and *huta,* which denotes the *root of trees or plants,* so that the compound *peźihuta,* which properly means medicine, [14] would signify literally *herbs* and *roots,* and *peźihutawićaśte* a *herb-and-root man;* which epithet is almost exclusively applied to American doctors resident in the vicinity of those Indians and to military surgeons at the forts in their territory. Among these people the gathering of herbs and root, and the administration of such medicines are, indeed, not in anywise uncommon; it is, however, not at all the occupation of men, but of women.

The word for *mouth* is *i*, whence is derived the verb *ia*, *to speak*, which in its turn gives rise (by the addition of the ending *pi* so common in the formation of verbal nouns) to the substantive *iapi, speech, language.* (Thus *Dakota iapi*, the Dakota language, properly the language of the *companions, friends*, or *allies.*)

The verb *ha* means to *curl.* It is also used with the reduplication, viz: *haha*, as an adjective especially, to denote *curling, curled.* The same when combined with *mini*, [15] *water*, signifies *curling* water; and thus *mini-haha* is the usual word for a *waterfall*, a *cascade* generally. Often *haha* alone is used to designate a *waterfall; mini* (water) being understood, just as we are accustomed in English to employ simply the word *"falls"* in the same sense. Thus the word *hahatuŋwe* is used, meaning *those who dwell or live at the falls, the people around the waterfalls*, an expression which has become among the Dakotas the ordinary name of the Chippewa Nation. [16]

To translate the word *minihaha* (or erroneously written *"Minnehaha"* by *laughing* waters, seems to be a gross mistake, most probably the result of imperfect information derived from some half-breed Sioux who was perhaps asked, (the inquirer wrongly analyzing the word,) "What is meant by *minne?*" To which the response was doubtless, "*Mini* means *water.*" "And what does *ihaha* signify?" The answer to which must have been: "*Ihaha* means to *laugh.*" (No doubt *i* signifying *mouth*, and *ha*, to *curl; iha* and *ihaha* mean *to curl the mouth or the lips,* that is, *to laugh.*) [17] When Rev. S. K. Riggs, in his otherwise very excellent Dakota Dictionary, explains *ihaha* by "*to laugh along as rapid water, the noise of waterfalls,*" [18] he is unconsciously led astray by that current popular error. In fact, such an interpretation is founded on nothing, and is *prima facie* quite contrary to all right etymology. [19] And to do justice to Mr. Riggs, for whom we profess the highest esteem, and who is without any comparison the best grammarian and lexicographer who has ever yet appeared in the domain of American Indian philology, we will state that he likewise explains (in his dictionary) ha-ha by "*waterfalls, so called from the* CURLING *waters.*"

Our views on this subject, as on various other similar matters, were, moreover, fully approved by Rev. T. S. Williamson, another distinguished missionary, and a highly respectable authority as regards the Dakota language, with whom we had many a long conversation on such topics every time we happened to meet with him in the territory.

Much might yet be done in investigating that most interesting language, in a *strictly philological* manner, and also tracing particularly the many Dakota names of mountains, hills, rivers, lakes, &c., to their true origin and meaning. They almost always contain some attractive allusion, something legendary or traditional, which might lead to most valuable results in regard to the history, religious ideas, ancient usages, &c., of this largest and most powerful of all the Indian tribes of North America.

We now say, in conclusion, that on *this* continent, researches in philology, ethnology, and history should have for their main object the languages and nations of AMERICA. The field is comparatively new and exceedingly interesting; an immense deal has to be done in this domain, the *real* labors of *thorough* and *exhaustive* investigation having not even yet begun. If these unpretending pages, contributed by the author as his first mite to that kind of research which he wishes to see undertaken by the scholars of this country, serve as an incentive to others to interest themselves in these studies and devote some of their time and exertions to the same, his object will have been successfully attained.

Notes

[1] Such intercalations are, in a measure, almost analogous to the usual insertion of the many incidental clauses in long Latin or German sentences, if we are allowed that comparison.

[2] ć stands in the present transcription of the Dakota language for *tch*; ś for *sh*; ŋ for *nasal n*; dotted letters indicate a peculiar emphasis in their utterance, for which we have no precise equivalent in English.

[3] Other examples in Mantchoo are kaka, meaning *male, cock,* while keke means *hen,* &c. These pheimmena are, in their last analysis, reducible to a fixed principle, which still prevails, to some extent, in the above-mentioned group of Asiatic languages, and which we have some reason to believe once formed an essential part of many other tongues. We might perhaps not improperly recognize in that antagonism something of *polar* opposition, some law of *polarity.* There are distinct and polarly opposite correlative vowel-classes, viz: *a, o, u,* in the continental pronunciation, which are, as it were, *positive,* and *e, i,* which are *negative.* Sometimes, however, the reverse takes place, so that *c, i,* have the power and significance of *a, o, u,* and *vice versa,* (a *quasi* "inversion of the poles.") This division is not an arbitrary one, but — we remark this by the way — the classification results quite naturally from a certain antagonistic relation of these vowels, respectively, to the guttural letters, their very test and touchstone. According to the nature of these vowels, the word receives often its characteristic meaning in those Asiatic languages; hence, only vowels of the same class occur in one and the same word. It would lead us too far from our present subject if we should now elucidate more fully the phenomenon under consideration. We wish to make only a few remarks more. This peculiarity extends to adjectives and to verbs — qualities, (positive or

negative, as the case may be,) actions, and states of being; even to postpositions, &c., (direction, tendency, &c.) We could, indeed, illustrate it by hundreds of examples, especially in the Central-Asiatic languages, even in the Celtic tongues, particularly the Irish. We might point out a very considerable number of such instances finally depending on a certain principle of vowel harmony. Even in our own ancient and modern languages we can now and then discover some slight and obscure vestiges of that pei'haps originally quite extensive phenomenon of significant vowel antagonism. For instance, in Latin, in *cal*-idus and *gel*-idus; perhaps, also, in the fundamental form homin and *fe*min, (implying hemin: f=h, as in Span, *h*embra;) &c., and other expressions of contrast, negation, or opposite tendencies generally. We also find in German st*u*mm and st*i*mm — referring to the voice or its absence; in English, the verbs to step and to stop, &c.

[4] Though it is almost evident that ćuŋ has not a separate and independent existence in the language, but is always found combined with pronominal suffixes, such as *ćuŋku, (her elder sister,)* we nevertheless meet also compounds like the following: *ćuŋya, to have for an elder sister.* We may, therefore, safely conclude that ćuŋ and the verb *ćuŋya* is the word which designates an elder sister. Moreover, the form *ćuŋku* has a parallel expression in *ćinću,* which means *his elder brother;* and as ću is identical with cm in consequence of a very common consonantal *permutation,* it becomes obvious that ćuŋ, indeed, means *elder sister,* as ćiŋ is known to signify *elder brother.*

[5] In the Grusinian language, *mama* means *father* — an apparent anomaly, owing, perhaps, to a mere interchange of the labials, passing here over into their extrenfes. Another shifting of the labials, though less in extent, we find in the Asiatic tongues, where we also meet with baba, for father, *fafa* for mother, &c.

[6] By means of such postpositions the declension of nouns is effected in the Ural-Altaic languages. The Dakota cases of declension, if we can use this term, amount likewise to a very rude sort of *ag-*

glutination, or rather simple adding of the postpositions to the nouns. There can be here no question of any *real* inflection or declension, since there is throughout only a kind of loose *ad*hesion, and nowhere what we might call a true *co*hesion. The postpositions are in the written language added to the nouns without being conjoined to them in writing, (except the plural ending *pi,*) as is also the case in the Mongolian language, the Turco-Tartar dialects, and other tongues of this class.

[7] We see in the historical development of our own modern languages an abundance of similar phenomena; thus in respect of the mere quasi-monumental, and, as it were, fossil existence of labials, such, for instance, as *b, p;* and in regard to English words like *debt,* which in French long ago became *dette.* In English the *b* of *debt* (== *debitum*) has become only silent, while in French, on the contrary, it has now no tolerance whatever, even as an historical landmark. There is, in fact, more conservatism in English. The French appears a more volatile, changeable element, even in the minor details of the language. Thus, again, we have in English the word *doubt,* with petrified silent *b,* which they seem unwilling, as yet, to let go, while in French we have *doute* without that *b.* Many other examples might be adduced in support of this very simple and common fact in all languages. In *sept,* (seven,) the French still neglect ridding their language of that now useless silent *p.* They do, it seems, not affect such antiquities, and will, most likely, do with words like *sept* as they have done with *clef,* (clavis,) where the final labial *f* became gradually *silent* but was *left* untouched. It is even *now* allowed to *remain,* but another form has already come into use at the same time with it, and a *key* is nowadays *clef* and *clé.*

[8] This interchange is seen in almost all languages of one and the same family, when compared with each other; thus, for instance, the use of *k* instead of *t* constitutes one of the characteristic differences between the Hawaiian tongue of the Sandwich Islands and the language of Tahiti, the Marquesas, Rarotangan, &c., *both*

groups, however, belonging to the Malayo-Oceanic, or more particularly the Micronesian stock.

[9] ć stands here for a letter that does not strictly belong to the word, viz. y, which is merely inserted euphonically between hokśi and opa.

[10] We venture this derivation so much tiie more boldly, inasmuch as the etymology of bread, brod, &c., is, in a degree, still an open question, Grimm connecting it — though not particularly insisting thereon — with brocken, brechen, to break, &c., while Anglo-Saxon scholars endeavor to trace the English word bread to breadan, (to nourish,) which, however, seems rather to be a denominative verb, such as lighten from light. Their etymological attempts being mere opinions, mere assertions without proof, we feel encouraged to maintain ours.

[11] The Greek is only an apparent exception to it, as is well understood by those conversant with the facts of comparative grammar.

[12] There is some room left for an attempt to derive wakaŋka direct from wakaŋ. The ideas possibly underlying such a derivation would appear to us rather far-fetched and fanciful.

[13] Other Indian tribes call alcoholic liquor fire-water instead of spirit-water, as, for instance, the Chippewas, in whose language it is ishkode wabu, &c.

[14] The word peźihuta is also applied to various other vegetable essences, beverages, &c. Thus, coffee is called peźihuta sapa, literally, black medicine; just as the Chippewas express it in their language by makade mashkiki wabu, (black medicine water.)

[15] The word mini (water) is the same which is contained also in the name of Minnesota, (properly mini-sota,) meaning whitish water, and referring to the Wakpa minisota, which is the Minnesota or St. Peter's River, and also to the Mde minisota, the so-called "Clear Lake."

[16] It is often the case that Indians give to other nations names simply derived from some entirely external, merely accidental, and altogether unessential circumstance or quality in these strangers,

which at first principally struck their attention. Thus, for instance, the inhabitants of the United States are called by the Dakotas *Isaŋtanka*, meaning *Big Knives;* by the Chippewas, *kitchimokoman,* which likewise signifies *Big Knives,* probably from the *swords* of the United States soldiers in the Territories.

[17] Just in the same way, the erroneous orthography of "Minnesota" was introduced for the more correct *Minisota;* and this is seen again — we mention it in passing — in that monstrous Dakota-Greek compound, "Minneapolis," meaning "*Water*town."

[18] Any such meanings of *ihaha,* as *"to bubble"* and making a noise like that of *waterfalls* must be considered simply as secondary, as a mere extension of the original signification of that word, viz. *laughing, i+haha,* mouth-curling, as it were; nothing whatever being contained in the constituents of that word which could have even the remotest reference to *water* or a *cascade.* The word itself seems to follow this deviation from its proper import, being even differently accentuated in that sort of figurative acceptation, viz. *ihaha* instead of *iháha.*

[19] Similar blunders frequently occur. Thus, in the erroneous and unmeaning English translation of Indian names generally — for instance, of "Hole-in-the-Day" — in which word it was intended to express simply one who (as a powerful archer) perforates the sky with his arrows, which we could easily place beyond any doubt, if it would not lead us too far from our present subject. So have travelers, too, themselves put the words "*squaw,*" "*papus,*" &c., into the mouths of the Dakotas, though these words belong exclusively to widely different tribes, and are on other occasions again repeated by the Dakota Indians to strangers, as they simply suppose such words to be English, and, therefore, more intelligible to the latter! The same applies to the Chippewa word "*nibo,*" (*he died* or *is dead,*) which travelers, probably deeming it the general and only *Indian* term for that idea, taught, as it were, to the Dakotas, who constantly make use of it in their conversation with Americans, mistaking it in

turn and in like manner for an English word, or something more easily accessible to the mind of the strangers.

Printed in the USA
CPSIA information can be obtained
at www.ICGtesting.com
LVHW040334201223
766964LV00007B/163